ITALIAN FOR BEGINNERS

15 Short Stories to Help You Learn and Enjoy Italian

Babel Publishing

Table of Contents

INTRODUCTION..1

HOW TO GET THE MOST OUT OF THIS BOOK..... 3

CAPITOLO 1: BUONGIORNO! 4

CAPITOLO 2: CHE FATICA IL LAVORO!................ 9

CAPITOLO 3: UNA NUOVA ESPERIENZA 14

CAPITOLO 4: MODELLA PER UN GIORNO.......... 20

CAPITOLO 5: L'INCONTRO 26

CAPITOLO 6: PROPOSTA DA PAZZI.................... 33

CAPITOLO 7: NORD E SUD 41

CAPITOLO 8: VIENI CON ME! 48

CAPITOLO 9: BENVENUTA A NAPOLI! 54

CAPITOLO 10: CHE MERAVIGLIA! 60

CAPITOLO 11: ALLEGRIA, SOLE.......................... 65

CAPITOLO 12: ...E MARE! 72

CAPITOLO 13: VIVI IL MOMENTO 80

CAPITOLO 14: UNA NUOVA OCCASIONE?.......... 88

CAPITOLO 15: ADDIO, MILANO! 94

CONCLUSION 101

Reading Comprehension And Quiz Keys 103

INTRODUCTION

Why do we love learning a new language? Each language is an open window to a different culture. The way people communicate says a lot about them. The sounds, intonations, sentence structures, the way words are built... every aspect of a language tells us much about a population. Speaking the local language in a foreign country allows you to build a stronger connection with its inhabitants, making your experience much deeper and more meaningful. There are so many reasons to challenge yourself with learning a new language.

This book is based on a true story. It is the story of a young Italian woman named Sara going about her day-to-day life in Italy. You are going to embark on a journey with her and experience her struggles, her dreams, her work, her interactions with other people, and many other aspects of her life.

Stories are a powerful tool when it comes to learning a new language. They are processed by our brains on a deeper level because they don't just deliver pieces of information, they stimulate our empathy, allowing us to get involved with the events and relate to the characters. We can often recognize parts of ourselves in these characters, which makes it easier to understand the different messages they try to convey, even if the language they use is different. Communication is not as much about grammar and vocabulary as it is about intent and tone, which most humans share and are able to recognize.

The aim of this book is to bypass the typical academic path to new languages and allow you to dive directly into an environment where Italian is spoken, thought, and felt. The whole book comprises 15 short stories about Sara and her life in Italy. Each short story comes with a set of comprehension exercises and quizzes on vocabulary and grammar that will guide you and help you understand the various parts of each chapter, while testing your newly formed language fundamentals.

You'll find a short word list at the end of each chapter, after the exercises, that can serve as a reference and covers hard-to-understand vocabulary.

Answers keys are provided at the end of the book, so you can see how well you did on each quiz. The vocabulary is simple, commonly used, and has many similarities to the English language. You will be amazed when you realize how much Italian you're able to understand right from the beginning!

Learning is about feelings: being able to understand feels rewarding, doesn't it? There's nothing better than a positive approach to help you fall in love with this fascinating language!

It's time to start... Coraggio!

HOW TO GET THE MOST OUT OF THIS BOOK

About 60% of the English vocabulary comes from Latin: the text takes largely advantage from the similarities between the two languages. Italian is read as it is written: when you don't know the meaning of a word, try to think about an English equivalent that can fit the situation.

This is far from a fantasy novel: it tells the story of a young girl living with a friend and earning her salary, who is offered a chance to change her life. It describes everyday situations she encounters and how she deals with them. Trust your intuition and play with your expectations. You'll probably get things right!

After reading each story, complete the reading comprehension section and quizzes to develop a better understanding of what you read. Be patient, and try to elaborate on the information given. Every effort you make will serve as a much more powerful memory tool then the simple use of a translator.

Words naturally repeat and you'll soon familiarize with a wider range of vocabulary, recognizing words you previously read and understood.

If you like, you can create your own list of words. It will work as a reference and grow over time!

And now... Cominciamo!

CAPITOLO 1: BUONGIORNO!

Il sole entra dalle grandi finestre e le campane suonano. Sono le 7, ma Sara è già sveglia da molto tempo. Sta lavando la sua tazza in cucina, quando Anna entra dalla porta assonnata.

"Buon... giorno... Sara..."

"Buongiorno Anna! Hai dormito bene?"

"...sì... Ho ancora sonno..."

"Ecco il caffé. Qui sul tavolo c'è la tua colazione."

"Grazie per il caffé! Che bello vivere con te. Ti svegli sempre presto e ogni mattina mi prepari la colazione."

"Non riesco a dormire fino a tardi. E mi piace alzarmi presto e vedere il sole, lo sai. Ho voglia di fare tutto con calma, soprattutto la colazione..."

"Non riesco a capire come riesci a mangiare le stesse cose che prepari al lavoro ogni giorno. Dopo un po' di tempo, a me non piacerebbero più..."

"Non c'è niente di meglio che svegliarsi e fare colazione con il cappuccino e la brioche! Poi il succo di arancia mi piace tantissimo!"

"Se lo dici tu..."

"La colazione è importante! Non sarebbe una buona giornata senza una buona colazione."

Le due amiche ridono insieme.

"Se lo dici tu... Ti invidio. Mangi tanti dolci eppure non ingrassi mai."

"Hai ragione, sono davvero fortunata. Ora vado in bagno, tra poco devo andare al lavoro!"

Sara si lava i denti e la faccia, si pettina i capelli e poi va in camera da letto per vestirsi.

Prende la borsa con le chiavi, il portafoglio e il cellulare ed esce di casa.

"Sei in ritardo!" le grida Anna.

"Lo so, lo so! Devo correre! Ultimamente non sono mai puntuale... Buona giornata!" grida Sara.

READING COMPREHENSION

1) Try to work the context out of the text! It's 7 am and Sara and Anna are having a typical Italian breakfast: coffee or cappuccino and a croissant/brioche with an orange juice.

2) Anna doesn't understand how Sara can eat the same things she makes at work every day. Where does Sara work?

3) There's a word that describes the relationship among the two girls in the text. Can you find it?

4) The text describes a typical morning on a workday. Sara performs very common actions before heading off to work. Can you find them in the text?

5) Scegli la giusta opzione per completare il riassunto.
Choose the right option to complete the summary.

Sara wakes up *early/late* in the morning. At 7, she's already up and makes breakfast for her flatmate, Anna. Anna doesn't understand how Sara can eat the same things she makes everyday at work, but Sara *just loves/is used to* her cappuccino and brioche in the morning. Sara goes out for work *early/late*, and Anna shouts at her she has to *hurry/relax* on her way to the café.

6) The following words are opposites. Can you work out their meaning from the text?
sveglia - assonnata
presto - tardi
puntuale - in ritardo

QUIZ

Choose the right answer among the options.

7) At 7, Sara is...
1. still sleeping
2. having breakfast
3. washing her cup

8) At 7, Anna is...
1. entering the kitchen
2. opening her eyes
3. rushing to work

9) Sara's favourite breakfast
1. depends on her mood
2. is cappuccino, croissant and orange juice
3. consists in a quick coffee

10) Anna says she envies Sara, because
1. She eats a lot, but never gets fat.
2. She likes waking up early in the morning.
3. She makes a better coffee than her.

VOCABULARY

sole - sun
finestra - window
sveglia - awake
tazza - cup
cucina - kitchen
porta - door
dormito - slept
bello - nice
vivere - live
colazione - breakfast
amiche - friends
ridono (inf.: ridere) - laugh
lava (inf.: lavare) - wash
denti - teeth
capelli - hair
vestirsi - dress up
borsa - bag
chiavi - keys
portafoglio - wallet
grida (inf.: gridare) - shout

CAPITOLO 2: CHE FATICA IL LAVORO!

Sara corre attraverso le vie e i parchi. Non sente i rumori delle auto che suonano il clacson quando attraversa la strada con il semaforo rosso.

Ultimamente è sempre in ritardo e questo è strano per lei.

Sa di essere responsabile e puntuale sul lavoro. E' felice di avere un'occupazione che le permette di guadagnare dei soldi per pagare l'affitto e il cibo e per uscire con gli amici.

Ma sa che i suoi ritardi significano che non è più felice di andare a lavorare al bar. Vorrebbe cambiare vita, trovare un altro impiego, ma ultimamente è difficile trovare un lavoro che sia soddisfacente. Non ha una laurea e ha sempre pensato di non poter desiderare di più, ma ultimamente si sveglia più tardi del solito ed è sempre in ritardo e questo non le piace.

In cinque minuti arriva alla porta del bar, sudata e in disordine. Il capo la guarda scuotendo la testa. Sara sorride, si scusa e ringrazia il capo per la sua pazienza. Corre in bagno a sistemarsi, spazza i pavimenti con la scopa e lava per terra. Pulisce velocemente il bancone e in poco tempo tutto è pronto per il servizio.

I clienti entrano uno dopo l'altro.
"Un caffè, grazie."
"Un succo di arancia."
"Un cappuccino e una brioche."
"Tre caffè, un espresso e due caffè lunghi."
"Un macchiato e un bicchiere d'acqua!"

La giornata procede senza sosta e presto si avvicina l'orario di chiusura. Sara non ha tempo di pensare a nulla quando lavora, è troppo impegnata.

Alle 16.30 comincia a pulire il locale e un'ora dopo, alle 17.30, si avvia verso casa. Ora che il lavoro è finito, a Sara ritornano in mente gli stessi pensieri.

"Ultimamente mi sento sempre stanca e fatico a sorridere con il cuore. Non sono mai stata una ritardataria, ma... Che fatica, svegliarsi la mattina. E pensare che mi piace così tanto svegliarmi presto, ma... Fatico seriamente a riconoscermi."

READING COMPREHENSION

1) Scegli la giusta opzione per completare il riassunto.
Choose the right option to complete the summary.

Sara hurries to *work/home*. She reflects on how unusual her behavior has been, lately. She is always *late/on time* for work, but she's usually *responsible and punctual/late*. She's *happy/tired* to have a job and a wage, but thinks about a change. She isn't serious though: it's *easy/hard* to find a decent job *with/without* a degree. She reaches the café, sweaty and *messy/tidy*. Her boss is disappointed. But Sara works hard and time *flies/goes slowly* by. As she goes back home, her mind is filled with *the same worries/thoughts* tormenting her in the morning.

2) Sara is an uncomplicated person: can you find a paragraph that describes her simple attitude to life?

3) A poetic word. Sara *wishes for* more - Sara *desidera* di più. The verb *DESIDERARE* comes from Latin: *de sidera*, which means "asking to the stars", referencing the soldiers who waited at the end of a day of battle for their companions to return to the camp. Now make a wish for yourself! *Io desidero...*

4) At work. What are Sara's main tasks at work? Find them in the text.
Her boss isn't happy to see her coming. What is the gesture that expresses his feelings?

5) At the café. You're now able to make simple orders: try to order a long coffee and a glass of orange juice!

6) Timetables. Italy uses a *24 hour* time system. What time does the service end? What time does Sara go out of the café and back home?

QUIZ

Are the following statements true or false? Mark V (vero) for true and F (falso) for false. Mark NS (non specificato) when not specified in the text.

7) Sara walks to work and she crosses the streets without watching, so the cars honk at her.
- V
- F
- NS

8) Sara wants to go to university.
- V
- F
- NS

9) Sara doesn't care if she's always late for work, in the last days.
- V
- F
- NS

10) Working hard helps Sara free her mind from thoughts.
- V
- F
- NS

11) Sara likes waking up early.
- V
- F
- NS

VOCABULARY

corre (inf.: correre)- run
rumori - noises
suonano (inf.: suonare) il clacson - honk
semaforo - traffic light
ultimamente - lately
permette (inf.: permettere) - allow
affitto - loan
cibo - food
uscire - go out
felice - happy
andare - go
impiego - employment
trovare - find
solito - usual
piace (inf.: piacere) - like
cinque - five
scuotendo (inf.: scuotere) - shake
testa - head
sorride (inf.: sorridere) - smile
spazza (inf.: spazzare) - sweep
pulisce (inf.: pulire) - clean
bancone - counter
pronto - ready
giornata - day
sosta - pause
impegnata - busy
stanca - tired
fatico (inf.: faticare) - have a hard time

CAPITOLO 3: UNA NUOVA ESPERIENZA

Sara sta per entrare dalla porta di casa, quando il cellulare suona improvvisamente.

"Pronto?"

"Ciao Sara, sono Simone. Come stai?"

"Tutto bene, Simone... nulla di nuovo. E tu, come stai?"

"Bene, bene... Ho bisogno di un favore. Lo studio fotografico per cui lavoro ha bisogno di modelli per una pubblicità. Siamo in ritardo su tutto... Abbiamo bisogno di ragazze e ragazzi. Domani sei libera? Hai voglia di fare la modella per un giorno?"

Sara è sorpresa, ma si ricorda che domani è il suo giorno libero.

"Sì, perché no! Sarà divertente."

"Grazie per l'aiuto, Sara. Ti devo un favore. Sarai pagata molto bene e non importa se non hai esperienza. Ti mando un messaggio con i dettagli sull'ora e il luogo dell'appuntamento."
"Grazie a te! Sono molto curiosa di scoprire il mondo della pubblicità. Buona serata Simone, a presto!"
"Buona serata a te! A presto!"

Sara si sveglia il giorno dopo e va all'appuntamento. Lo studio fotografico si trova in una zona che non conosce e Sara chiede indicazioni ai passanti.

"Mi scusi, che autobus devo prendere per andare alla stazione di Porta Genova?"
"La linea 65. La fermata si trova alla prossima via a destra."
"Grazie! In che direzione va l'autobus?"
"Prenda l'autobus in direzione Porta Genova. E' l'ultima fermata, non può sbagliare!"
"Perfetto! Buona giornata!"

Sara arriva alla stazione e chiede ancora indicazioni.

"Buongiorno. Devo andare in Via Firenze, numero 35. In che direzione devo andare?"
"E' qui vicino. Prenda la prima via a sinistra, poi giri alla seconda via a destra. Ci sono molti palazzi, stia attenta a trovare quello giusto."

Sara segue le indicazioni e attraversa vie piene di palazzi e grattacieli alti. Le sembrano tutti uguali, ma alla fine vede una ragazza bionda e molto bella fuori da un edificio.
Si avvicina a lei e si presenta.

"Ciao, piacere di conoscerti, sono Sara. Sei una modella? Lo studio fotografico è qui?"

"Ciao, piacere, sono Debora. Sì, tra poco arrivano i fotografi. Anche tu sei una modella?"
"No, faccio la barista, ma sono qui per fare un piacere a un amico..."

In pochi minuti arrivano i fotografi e i tecnici, insieme a molti ragazzi e ragazze. Sara si guarda attorno, è curiosa. Le sembrano tutti bellissimi e si sente disorientata.

Lo studio è un edificio grande, alto, bianco e luminoso. Sara si guarda intorno, ma il suo amico non c'è.

READING COMPREHENSION

1) Scegli la giusta opzione per completare il riassunto.
Choose the right option to complete the summary.

Sara is just *outside/inside* home, when her mobile suddenly rings. It's Simone, *a friend/her boyfriend*, asking her a favor. He's a photographer and needs a model for a simple shooting work the next day. Sara is *free from/busy with* work, so she *declines/accepts*. She will be *well/poorly* paid. Sara goes to the appointment and asks for directions. She takes the *train/bus* and then walks past tall buildings until she notices a *beautiful/simple* girl and introduces to her. They wait together for the photographers and the other models to arrive. Sara takes a look around and *finds/can't find* Simone.

2) Phone call. Simone and Sara have a quick phone call. How do you answer at the phone? How do you translate: "How are you? I'm fine."

3) Asking for directions. Sara asks for directions to reach her destination. How do you translate:
- "Which bus should I take to get to...?"
- Bus stop
- "Which direction should I take?"
- "Take the first street on the left."
- "Turn right on the second street."

4) Introduce yourself. Following Sara and Debora's example, introduce yourself and say what is your job.

5) Feelings. Underline the adjectives that refer to Sara's feelings and try to work out their meaning from the context.

QUIZ

Are the following statements true or false? Mark V (vero) for true and F (falso) for false. Mark NS (non specificato) when not specified in the text.

6) Sara has always wanted to be a model.
- V
- F
- NS

7) Sara has to get a permission from her boss to accept Simone's proposal.
- V
- F
- NS

8) Sara needs previous experience to work as a model.
- V
- F
- NS

9) Debora is a bartender, not a professional model.
- V
- F
- NS

10) Sara loves to be surrounded by beautiful people.
- V
- F
- NS

VOCABULARY

improvvisamente - suddenly

bisogno - need

pubblicità - advertisement

ricorda (inf.: ricordare) - remember

divertente - fun

devo (inf.: dovere) - owe

importa (inf.: importare) - matter

mondo - world

serata - evening

sbagliare - make mistakes

vicino - near

grattacieli - skyscrapers

piacere - favor

guarda (inf.: guardare) - look

attorno - around

CAPITOLO 4: MODELLA PER UN GIORNO

Sara nota che tutti hanno grandi borse e valigie. Pensa che i modelli vengano da altre parti d'Italia, ma poi capisce che non è così...

"Ciao, come ti chiami?" le chiede una make-up artist.
"Ciao, sono Sara. Sei una truccatrice?"
"Sì. Piacere, Sara, mi chiamo Marina. Hai portato dei vestiti?"
"No, non pensavo di dover portare altri vestiti... Ecco perché tutti hanno borse e valigie! Pensavo venissero da lontano."

Marina ride.

"No, no... Ma non è un problema. Chiediamo a qualcuno di prestarti dei vestiti e delle scarpe... Quello che indossi non va bene." dice la truccatrice, guardando i jeans, la maglietta e le sneakers di Sara con occhio critico.

Marina dà a Sara dei pantaloni stretti, una maglietta larga e delle scarpe con tacchi molto alti.

"Cambiati i vestiti in bagno e fammi vedere se ti stanno bene."

Sara guarda le scarpe con terrore. Non è abituata a camminare sui tacchi alti, ma rimane in silenzio e va a cambiarsi.
Si infila la maglietta e i pantaloni in fretta, poi infila le scarpe e cammina avanti e indietro per cinque minuti, fino a quando si sente sicura.
Torna da Marina camminando meglio che può.

"Perfetta! I vestiti ti stanno benissimo! Le scarpe sono del numero giusto?"
"Sì, sono 38. Non indosso mai i tacchi e faccio fatica a camminare... Ma il problema è mio, non delle scarpe!"
"E invece sembra che le indossi da sempre!"

Marina trucca Sara e poi le dice di andare nella stanza del fotografo.

L'ambiente è molto grande e il fotografo spiega a tutti il lavoro.

"Il nostro cliente è il produttore di un programma televisivo di musica. Voi marciate per i diritti della musica, camminate per le strade con in mano questi strumenti musicali e cantate, urlate, suonate...con energia!"

I ragazzi e le ragazze si mettono in fila davanti a un pannello bianco. Sara cerca di nascondersi dietro a Debora, ma il fotografo le chiede di spostarsi davanti a lei e Debora la guarda male, infastidita.

"Al mio via, correte verso l'obiettivo. Mi raccomando: con energia!"

Sara si guarda intorno, disorientata. Pensa: "Correre? Con i tacchi... no, per favore! Questo no!"
Ma non ha neanche il tempo di pensare.

"Uno, due, tre... via!"

Gli scatti proseguono e Sara si diverte. Il fotografo mostra a tutti le fotografie e indica proprio Sara come esempio.

"Vedete? Lei è grintosa, arrabbiata, ma anche divertita! Così! Energia!"

Arriva presto l'ora di pranzo e nella sala a fianco è imbandito un lungo tavolo pieno di cibo.
Sara non crede ai suoi occhi: ha molta fame e davanti a lei ci sono caffé, croissant per tutti i gusti e moltissimi sandwich.
Solo pochi si avvicinano al tavolo. Sara ne approfitta e riempie il suo piatto.
Mangia, torna al tavolo, riempie il piatto e mangia ancora con gusto.

Poi torna di nuovo al tavolo e sente un ragazzo ridere al suo fianco. "Hai fame, eh? E' incredibile. Mangi tantissimo eppure sei così magra!"

READING COMPREHENSION

1) Scegli la giusta opzione per completare il riassunto.
Choose the right option to complete the summary.

The models carry *big suitcases/small bags* with them. Sara thinks they come from *abroad/other parts of Italy*. Marina is a make-up artist and gives Sara *advice on how/clothes* to dress. Sara feels *uncomfortable/ok* with high-heeled shoes. Marina puts make-up on Sara and invites her to the next room. There the photographer explains the job: the models have to pretend to be *passing by/marching* and playing *a song/musical instruments*. They have to *run/walk slowly* towards the camera. The photographer is *satisfied with/unhappy* about Sara. At lunch break, there's a *lot/little* food. Sara serves *three times/twice* and a boy notices she eats a lot.

2) What's inside the models' bags?

3) What happens between Sara and Debora? Why is Debora annoyed?

4) How do you translate: "One, two, three... go!"

5) What does the photographer like about Sara?

6) Clothes. Find the following words and expressions in the text:
t-shirt - The clothes really suit you! - wear/put on - shoes - high heels - trousers

QUIZ

Choose the right answer among the options.

7) Marina's task is
1. to put make-up on people.
2. to choose the right clothes for the models.
3. to dress and put make-up on the models.

8) The photographer wants the models to be _____, first of all.
1. good actors
2. energetic
3. good musicians

9) The clothes Sara wears at first are
1. uncomfortable.
2. too casual.
3. well matched.

10) Sara can walk well on high heels, because
1. she leans against the wall.
2. she usually wears this kind of shoes.
3. she tries her best.

11) At lunch, Sara
1. isn't hungry.
2. eats with pleasure.
3. doesn't love the food.

VOCABULARY

capisce (inf: capire) - understand
portato - brought
occhio - eye
stretti - tight
larga - large
abituata - used
fretta - hurry
avanti e indietro - back and forth
può (inf.: potere) - can
giusto - right
nostro - our
diritti - rights
in fila - in a row
neanche - even
grintoso - gutsy
arrabbiata - furious
imbandito - prepared
crede (inf.: credere) - believe
tutti - all
gusti - tastes
approfitta (inf.: approfittare) - take advantage
riempie (inf.: riempire) - fill
fianco - side

CAPITOLO 5: L'INCONTRO

Sara toglie gli occhi dal piatto e guarda il ragazzo che le ha parlato. Ride e risponde:
"Lo so, non sei l'unico che me lo dice... Sono fortunata, lo so!"

"Piacere, sono Roberto. Non so come fai a correre su quei tacchi, sono altissimi..."
"Sono Sara, piacere! E' la prima volta che metto dei tacchi così alti. Quando ho indossato le scarpe, avevo il terrore di cadere, ma in realtà non è difficile stare in piedi."
"Se lo dici tu..."
"Certo che anche tu mangi tantissimo, eppure sei magro... Credo che qui siamo gli unici affamati!"

Sara e Roberto si siedono a un tavolino e mangiano insieme. Ma la pausa pranzo finisce presto e il fotografo chiama tutti per continuare con gli scatti.

Qualche ora più tardi, le segretarie chiedono a tutti i dati personali: nome, cognome, indirizzo e numero di telefono.

Fuori dallo studio, tutti si salutano e tornano a casa.

Sara rientra a casa e subito Anna le chiede come è andata, è curiosa.

"Bene, bene, mi sono divertita! Ho dovuto camminare su dei tacchi altissimi..." ride.

"Non ti immagino proprio!" ride Anna. "E... hai conosciuto qualche bel ragazzo?"

"...in realtà, sì. C'era un grande buffet e puoi immaginare: ho mangiato tantissimo! Che meraviglia!"

"Questo è proprio da te. Ma ti ho chiesto dei ragazzi, non del cibo!"

"Sì, sì, giusto. Al tavolo, alla fine, eravamo solo io e Roberto... Si è divertito quando ha visto che mangiavo tanto e si è presentato."

"Ah, davvero? E com'è lui?"

"E' alto, con i capelli e gli occhi scuri. Ha delle labbra carnose e un viso davvero bellissimo. Stavo per prendermi un colpo appena mi sono girata a guardarlo!"

"Ma che fortuna... Vi siete scambiati i contatti?"

"No, è un peccato..."

"Pensi solo a mangiare!" risponde Anna, ridendo.

Il giorno dopo, Sara è di nuovo al lavoro. Ma è meno concentrata del solito: fa errori continuamente e il capo la osserva, scuotendo la testa più del solito.

Sara ha solo un pensiero in testa: il ragazzo che ha conosciuto il giorno prima. Continua a chiedersi come fare per ritrovarlo.

L'orario di chiusura arriva più presto del solito e Sara si avvia sulla strada di casa.

Questa volta non è preoccupata, cammina tranquilla e con la testa tra le nuvole.

Il cellulare squilla sulla porta di casa: è un numero che non conosce.

"Può mai essere lui...? Meglio non farsi illusioni" pensa, e risponde.

"Buonasera, polizia. Parlo con Sara?"

"Polizia? Sì, sono Sara... E' successo qualcosa?"

Sara è preoccupata. Ma ha dei dubbi: perchè la polizia la chiama per nome? E quella voce... le ricorda qualcuno.

READING COMPREHENSION

1) Scegli la giusta opzione per completare il riassunto.
Choose the right option to complete the summary.

Roberto introduces to Sara and notices she *is beautiful/eats a lot*. They sit together and talk for *long/just a bit*, then they go back to work. When they finish, everyone *goes straight back home/leave their personal data and go home*. Anna asks Sara about *her day/Roberto*. Sara says she *had fun/is tired* and tells her flatmate about *Simone/Roberto*. The next day, Sara is *concentrated/distracted* at work. She thinks about the *future/boy she met*. As she walks home, she is *worried/thoughtful*. She receives a call from an unknown number: it's *a friend/the police*.

2) Movements. Try to find the following expressions in the text. They all refer to Sara on high heels...
walk - run - stand - fall

3) Sara and Roberto have one thing in common. Can you tell what it is?

4) Personal data. Try to fill out this form with your personal data.
Nome _____ Cognome _____ Indirizzo _____
Numero di telefono _____

5) Sara really likes Roberto. She uses the colloquial expression: *"Stavo per prendermi un colpo"*, that can be translated as: "I was about to get a stroke", to say that she was deeply surprised to see such a handsome boy talking to her.

6) Sara focuses her description on a particular part of Roberto's body. Can you tell what it is?

7) Sara receives a call from the police, but something sounds strange. Can you tell what it is?

QUIZ

Choose the right answer among the options.

8) Roberto introduces himself to Sara...
  1) on the set.
  2) just outside the studio.
  3) at the lunch table.

9) Sara tells Anna first
  1) about walking on high heels.
  2) about Roberto.
  3) about the food.

10) Anna says Sara is more interested in _____ than boys.
  1) high heels
  2) food
  3) work

11) At work, time seem...
  1) to fly by.
  2) to pass slowly.
  3) to stop.

12) As she hears the phone ringing, Sara thinks _____ is calling.
  1) the police
  2) Roberto
  3) Anna

VOCABULARY

toglie (inf.: togliere) - move away
so (inf.: sapere) - know
prima - first
volta - time
credo (inf.: credere) - believe
qui - here
scatti - shootings
fuori - outside
salutano (inf.: salutare) - say hi/goodbye
rientra (inf.: rientrare) - come back
proprio - exactly
fine - end
labbra - lips
appena - as/in the moment
di nuovo - again
meglio - better

CAPITOLO 6:
PROPOSTA DA PAZZI

La voce al telefono **tace**. Sara è sempre più sospettosa.

"Pronto? Pronto, <u>mi</u> sente? E' successo qualcosa?" **chiede**.

Sente una risata dall'altra parte.

"Sara, sono Roberto! Non dirmi che hai creduto allo scherzo."

Il cuore <u>le</u> si ferma. Resta un momento in silenzio, poi **esclama**: "Roberto, ciao! Sì, ci avevo creduto... I vicini di casa si **lamentano** sempre dei rumori delle feste che organizziamo durante il fine settimana, magari questa volta avevano chiamato la polizia..."
"<u>Ti</u> piace divertirti, vero?"
"Roberto... come hai trovato il mio numero?"

"Ricordi? A fine giornata ci hanno chiesto i dati personali e il numero. Ho ascoltato mentre lo **dettavi**..." **dice** il ragazzo, a voce bassa.

Sara è felice, **domanda**: "Ma non era meglio chiederlo a me?"

"L'importante è averti trovata. E poi sembravi davvero spaventata quando ti ho detto che ero un poliziotto. E' stato divertente!"

"Che pazzo."

"A proposito di pazzia, ti va di uscire a bere un caffè insieme a me?"

"Certo!"

"Bene, non sono l'unico pazzo. Perfetto. Allora va bene se ci vediamo domani a quest'ora? Conosci il Gran Caffé in Piazza Garibaldi?"

"Sì, domani a quest'ora va benissimo e conosco il bar. Ci vediamo domani!"

"A domani, Sara. Buona serata!"

Sara è al settimo cielo e **racconta** tutto ad Anna.

"Sembra proprio un tipo simpatico. Che fortuna! Sono proprio felice per te."

"Sì, sono impaziente di conoscerlo. Oggi al lavoro avevo in testa solo lui... ho rotto tazze, sbagliato in cassa e ho perfino versato un caffè sulla giacca di un signore elegante. Il mio capo sembrava infuriato."

Anna ride. "Attenta, pensa a una cosa alla volta altrimenti al posto di tagliare il pane finirai per tagliarti un dito!"

Sara si sveglia la mattina dopo, più presto del solito e piena di energia.

Va al lavoro saltellando, cantando per la strada. Il capo si meraviglia: la ragazza è in anticipo e lavora concentrata, con energia. Anche il suo sorriso sembra molto più sincero.

Al momento della chiusura, Sara pulisce il locale in un attimo e corre a casa a prepararsi.
Guarda i suoi vestiti scuotendo la testa: ha solo magliette e vestiti sportivi e comodi. Poi il viso le si illumina: guarda nell'ultimo cassetto e tira fuori l'unico vestito elegante che ha. Soddisfatta, lo indossa e va all'appuntamento.

Roberto la aspetta appena fuori dal bar. Appena la vede, scoppia a ridere e le dice che sembra una vecchia signora, vestita così elegante.

"Pensavo fossi più il tipo da vestiti sportivi..."
Sara è delusa, ma si **giustifica** e **spiega**: "Tra i tacchi alti e i vestiti eleganti, non mi crederesti se ti dico che invece sono proprio come dici tu!"

READING COMPREHENSION

1) Scegli la giusta opzione per completare il riassunto.
Choose the right option to complete the summary.

Roberto called Sara pretending to be *her neighbor/the police*. Sara *is happy and/is nervous but* doesn't get angry about the joke. The boy asks her to go out *the next day/the day after tomorrow* for a *coffee/meal* at a *restaurant/café* they both know. Sara accepts right away and tells everything to Anna. The next day, at work, she's *very concentrated/even less concentrated*, which makes her boss *happy/discontent*. She goes back home and gets ready for the date. She looks for an elegant dress and finds it *right away/in the last drawer*. Roberto laughs about her *dress/hairstyle*.

2) Can you explain the title of the chapter? What's the meaning of the adjective *"pazzo"*? Can you find its corresponding noun form?

3) Personal pronouns. Fill in the gaps in the table using the underlined particles in the text.

SUBJECT	OBJECT
I - io	me -___
you - tu	you -___
he/she - lui/lei	him/her - lo/___
we - noi	us -___
you - voi	you - vi
they - loro	them - si

4) Conversation. Try to match the corresponding verbs in Italian, scanning the text and choosing among the words in bold.

stop talking - ask - say - exclaim - complain - dictate - ask - tell - justify - explain

5) Sara is truly happy after the call. She's "in seventh heaven:" find the Italian corresponding expression in the text.

6) Sara is an open book: one can tell her feelings by looking at her behavior. What does she do when she feels joyful?

7) Sara's attitude on the workplace is affected by her feelings, as well. What does she do when she's full of thoughts? How does she work when her mind is free?

8) Things are not as they seem at first: this expression can relate to Sara and Roberto's interactions twice. Can you tell when each of them believe something that reveals to be wrong?

QUIZ

Choose the right answer among the options.

9) Sara falls for Roberto's joke because
  1) she was caught stealing.
  2) her neighbors complain about the noise during the weekend.
  3) she was expecting a call from the police.

10) Roberto knows Sara's number, because
  1) he looked it up in a phone book.
  2) he eavesdropped it.
  3) he asked her.

11) Roberto and Sara will meet
  1) later in the day, in Piazza Garibaldi.
  2) after work, at Sara's.
  3) after work, in Piazza Garibaldi.

12) When Anna hears about Sara's news, she's
  1) envious.
  2) indifferent.
  3) happy for her.

13) As Sara tells her friend she's been inattentive at work, Anna recommends her
  1) not to cut her fingers instead of the bread.
  2) not to pour coffee on the clients' jacket.
  3) not to think about Roberto.

14) Sara's smile changes: it's
  1) brighter.
  2) more sincere.
  3) fake.

15) Sara's wardrobe is full of
    1) clothes she doesn't need.
    2) comfortable sports clothes.
    3) elegant dresses.

16) As the closing time approaches, Sara
    1) goes home earlier than usual.
    2) hurries with the cleaning and runs home.
    3) thinks about the boy she's going to meet.

17) Sara justifies with Roberto about
    1) being late.
    2) her elegant dress.
    3) her messy hair.

VOCABULARY

sempre - always/increasingly
qualcosa - something
magari - maybe
vero - true
simpatico - nice
rotto (inf.: rompere) - break
versato (inf.: versare) - pour
altrimenti - otherwise
saltellando - jumping
attimo - moment
vecchia - old
delusa - disappointed

CAPITOLO 7: NORD E SUD

I due ragazzi entrano nel bar e ordinano al cameriere due caffè.

Parlano con calma e si sentono a loro agio, si guardano negli occhi mentre si raccontano le loro storie.

Sara scopre che Roberto non è un modello: anche per lui era la prima volta davanti a un fotografo.
"Se non sei un modello, che lavoro fai?"
"Lavoro nel settore delle risorse umane, selezione del personale. Sono laureato in Legge."
"Ah, che bello! Mi sarebbe piaciuto molto studiare all'Università, ma ho dovuto lasciare il corso dopo due anni per cominciare a lavorare."

"Che lavoro fai? E cosa hai studiato all'Università?"
"Faccio la barista in un locale qui a Milano. Ho studiato lingue straniere: inglese, tedesco, spagnolo... qualche volta le uso con i clienti del bar e mi diverto."

"Non hai mai pensato di fare la traduttrice?"

"E' molto difficile trovare un lavoro senza una laurea. Ho una grande passione per le lingue straniere, ma ogni volta che mando curricula per tradurre non ricevo risposta, mi ignorano completamente."

"Posso capire... Nel Sud Italia è ancora più difficile e mi sento fortunato ad avere un buon lavoro."

"Nel Sud Italia? Non lavori qui?"

"No, sono qui di passaggio. Ho molti amici a Milano perchè ho fatto un Master qui, dopo la laurea. A volte vengo a trovarli e mi ospitano per un po' di tempo."

"Dove vivi?"

"A Napoli. E' bella, la mia città natale. Sono molto affezionato alle mie radici. Sono felice di avere un lavoro laggiù, preferisco Napoli a Milano. La storia, le persone, il clima, il mare..."

"Non avrei mai detto che sei di Napoli, non hai un minimo di accento!"

"Tu invece parli proprio come una milanese" risponde Roberto, imitando l'accento lombardo.

Il ragazzo spiega che il giorno dopo prenderà il treno di ritorno. Sara sembra triste, ma Roberto le fa una proposta inaspettata.

"Hai mai visto Napoli? Vorrei mostrarti la città. Se ne parla tanto e male, ma ha i suoi lati positivi e voglio farteli scoprire. Perchè non prendi il treno insieme a me?"

READING COMPREHENSION

1) Put the sentences in the right order to obtain a short summary of the chapter.

a) Sara talks about her job and her studies.
b) Roberto mocks Sara's accent.
c) Sara and Roberto sit in the café and start talking.
d) Roberto talks about his recruitment job and his degree.
e) Roberto talks about his native town.
f) Roberto asks Sara to take the train with him the following day.
g) They feel at ease and look in each other's eyes while telling their stories.

2) Looking for a job. Find the following expressions in the text:
what is your job? - start working - I work in the human resource sector - I send CVs - I'm a bartender - don't you work here? - what did you study? - to have a good job

3) Where does Sara live? Where does Roberto come from?

4) Roberto loves his native town. What does he like about it, in particular?

5) Italian regional accents. Every region in Italy has their own dialect and accent. From North to South, from one region to another, differences can be huge. Edoardo Mecca is a popular Italian YouTuber who paid homage to the Italian peninsula with a nice video: "Il giro d'Italia in due minuti" (A two-minutes tour in Italy). If you're curious about Italian accents, take a look! He'll be talking very fast, but you'll be able to catch some words and hear how Italian sounds in all regions, in this order: Valle d'Aosta, Piemonte, Liguria, Lombardia (Milan), Trentino, Friuli, Veneto, Emilia Romagna, Toscana, Umbria, Marche, Abruzzo, Campania (Naples), Basilicata, Puglia, Calabria, Sicilia and Sardegna.

QUIZ

Choose the right answer among the options.

6) The chapter is called "North and South", because
1) Roberto and Sara talk about the differences between North and South Italy.
2) Roberto and Sara come from different parts of Italy.
3) Roberto and Sara travelled through Italy.

7) Roberto works as a
1) model.
2) recruitment agent.
3) barman.

8) Sara left her studies at the University, because
1) she had to start working.
2) she didn't like foreign languages.
3) she wasn't good enough.

9) Sara thinks she can't work as a translator, because
1) she can't speak foreign languages well enough.
2) the job is too complicated.
3) she doesn't have a degree.

10) Roberto went to Milan
1) to visit friends.
2) to look for a job.
3) to visit his family.

11) Roberto got his master's degree in
1) Milan.
2) his home town.
3) a foreign country.

12) Roberto likes his home town, but there's a negative side to it:
1) the climate.
2) the lack of jobs.
3) the people.

13) Who has the strongest accent?
1) Sara
2) Roberto
3) none of them

14) Roberto is going back to his home town
1) later in the evening
2) in the weekend
3) the next morning

15) Roberto wants to show Sara his home town
1) to show her the best sides of an often-belittled city.
2) to go bathing in the sea.
3) to introduce her to his family.

VOCABULARY

cameriere - waiter
sentono (inf.: sentire) - feel
loro - their
tedesco - German
qualche volta - sometimes
radici - roots
imitando (inf.: imitare) - mock
sembra (inf.: sembrare) - look (like)
perchè - why

CAPITOLO 8:
VIENI CON ME!

Sara vorrebbe accettare subito la proposta: non ha mai visto Napoli e le piace viaggiare, ma soprattutto non vuole rinunciare a Roberto. Ma il suo senso di responsabilità prevale sulle ragioni del cuore: ha un lavoro e non vuole avere problemi.
Rifiuta, riluttante.

Ma Roberto insiste: "Puoi dire al tuo capo che sei malata e stare con me solo per pochi giorni. Sei stata così pazza da accettare il mio invito, ti chiedo un'ultima pazzia: vieni con me! Ti prometto che non te ne pentirai."

Sara è sempre più indecisa e Roberto la convince. Ma ha paura che la ragazza cambi idea, così le chiede di chiamare subito il suo capo.

"Pronto? Sara?"

"Sì, buonasera capo. Scusi se la chiamo a quest'ora, ma volevo avvisarla che ho preso una brutta influenza e ho la febbre alta. Il dottore mi ha raccomandato di rimanere a casa dal lavoro per almeno un paio di giorni, ma tornerò non appena mi sento meglio."

"Ultimamente eri proprio strana, forse stavi per ammalarti... Capisco. Va bene. Avvisami non appena ti senti meglio. A presto, riguardati!"

"Grazie capo. Buona serata, a presto."

Sara si sente in colpa, ma tutti i dubbi svaniscono non appena vede il sorriso di Roberto.

"Grazie, Sara! Sono davvero felice che tu sia così pazza! Vedrai, non te ne pentirai!"

A casa, Sara comunica ad Anna la sua decisione.

"Quel ragazzo mi piace ancora di più. E' proprio il tipo ideale per te. Sei molto responsabile, ma non ti godi abbastanza la vita. Insomma, che bella notizia! Mandami qualche foto, mi raccomando!"

"Grazie, Anna... Anche io sono davvero felice della mia decisione! Sono impaziente di vedere Napoli!"

"Napoli è solo una scusa!" ride Anna. "Piuttosto... chi mi preparerà la colazione? Mi mancherai."

Sara fatica ad addormentarsi. Punta la sveglia per il giorno dopo, ma ha paura di non sentirla e alla fine passa la notte in bianco per l'agitazione.

Si presenta in stazione molto presto e Roberto si preoccupa quando la vede.

"Ehi, che faccia... Non dirmi che hai preso davvero l'influenza!"

READING COMPREHENSION

1) Choose the right alternative to complete the summary.

a) Sara *accepts right away/lets Roberto convince her*.
b) She calls her boss and tells him she *got a bad flu/doesn't want to work tomorrow*.
c) Sara's doubts disappear, when *her boss doesn't complain/she sees Roberto's smile*.
d) Anna thinks Sara *doesn't enjoy her life enough/is reckless*.
e) Anna will miss Sara *preparing her breakfast/waking her up in the morning*.
f) Sara sets the alarm clock *and sleeps well/but can't sleep*.
g) Roberto is worried, because *Sara's face looks terrible/Sara is late*.

2) A hard choice. Sara experiences a range of feelings when making her choice. Find the related terms in the text and link them with their English translations:

reluctant - uncertain - feels guilty - doubts - happy - impatient

3) A fake illness. Sara makes up an excuse to skip work, pretending to feel sick. Read her conversation with the boss again and underline the terms related to health.

4) Passare la notte in bianco. This expression can be literally translated with "pass the night in white" and means "staying up all night". This way of saying comes from the Middle Age, when knights had to stay up all night the day before their initiation. They dressed in white, fasted and reflected upon their duties and the history of the order they were about to join.

QUIZ

Are the following statements true or false? Mark V (vero) for true and F (falso) for false. Mark NS (non specificato) when not specified in the text.

5) Sara is torn between her duties and the reasons of her heart.
- V
- F
- NS

6) Sara doesn't love travelling.
- V
- F
- NS

7) Roberto asks Sara to do something crazy for the last time.
- V
- F
- NS

8) Roberto wants Sara to call her boss right away, to prevent her from changing her mind.
- V
- F
- NS

9) Sara tells her boss she has a severe migraine.
- V
- F
- NS

10) Sara's boss gets angry at the phone.
- V
- F
- NS

11) Anna thinks Roberto and Sara are different.
- V
- F
- NS

12) Anna understands Sara's desire to visit Naples is just an excuse.
- V
- F
- NS

13) Sara can't sleep because she fears she won't hear the alarm ringing in the morning.
- V
- F
- NS

14) Roberto thinks Sara truly caught a flu.
- V
- F
- NS

VOCABULARY

subito - right away
soprattutto - most of all
pochi - a few
almeno - at least
non appena - as soon as
stavi per (inf.: stare per) - be going to
riguardati (inf: riguardarsi) - take care
ancora di più - even more
mandami (inf.: mandare) - send
presto - soon

CAPITOLO 9:
BENVENUTA A NAPOLI!

La preoccupazione di Roberto svanisce presto. Sara comincia a sbadigliare non appena si siede e, poco dopo, si addormenta. Il ragazzo capisce che non ha dormito e la sveglia solo quando il treno arriva a destinazione.

Sara è imbarazzata e si scusa, ma Roberto le dice di non preoccuparsi.
Si è divertito molto a osservare le sue espressioni durante il sonno e ha dovuto trattenersi dal farle qualche scherzo.

Non appena scendono dal treno, si sente il suono di un clacson. E' l'addetto alla pulizia delle banchine che cerca di passare in mezzo alla folla di viaggiatori.

Sara scoppia a ridere: "Sembra una di quelle barzellette piene di pregiudizi su Napoli! Tutti che suonano, gridano... Non ci posso credere! Appena metto piede fuori dal treno... BEEP!"

Roberto si offende, le risponde che Napoli è piena di vita... e di senso civico e rispetto, a suo modo.

Non appena i due salgono in macchina, Sara ride ancora mentre Roberto sfreccia nel mezzo del traffico.

"Non riuscirei mai a guidare qui."
"Basta evitare ogni indecisione che rallenti il traffico... la precedenza si prende e basta, senza stare a pensarci. Il numero di incidenti, qui, è di molto inferiore rispetto a Milano..."

Sara pensa che Roberto non ha tutti i torti. Le macchine sfrecciano senza badare troppo alle regole della strada, ai sensi di marcia e ai divieti, ma lasciano passare i pedoni senza suonare e senza arrabbiarsi, mentre a Milano gli automobilisti sono meno tolleranti verso le persone a piedi.

La ragazza rimane incantata dalla natura e dai palazzi antichi che passano fuori dal finestrino, mentre Roberto la conduce verso la parte alta della città.

Ferma l'auto ad una salita panoramica e Sara rimane a bocca aperta. Davanti ai suoi occhi si allarga la città, un vulcano, il mare e le isole. Roberto le indica una lunga via che sembra dividere a metà lo scenario.

"Vedi quella lunga strada? Si chiama Spaccanapoli perché va da una parte all'altra della città e la divide perfettamente."

Sara è entusiasta, vorrebbe esplorare tutto.

"Non hai ancora visto niente... E poi ricordati che dobbiamo pranzare! Vedrai... qui si mangia davvero bene e si spende poco, altro che a Milano! Qualità al giusto prezzo!" scherza, mimando uno slogan pubblicitario.

READING COMPREHENSION

1) Scegli la giusta opzione per completare il riassunto.
Choose the right option to complete the summary.

Roberto's worries disappear when Sara falls asleep *almost immediately/after a while*. He wakes her up *when they arrive at their destination/middleway*. As they get off the train, Sara hears *a honk/people talking loud* and is amused by the fact she *didn't expect that/expected that*. Roberto *laughs/feels offended*. Sara is amused by Roberto's *fast and reckless/calm and cautious* driving, as well. He justifies by telling her that Neapolitan drivers are more respectful of *traffic laws/pedestrians* and car accidents are *lower/higher* there than in Milan. Roberto drives to the *higher/lower* part of the city and Sara enjoys the amazing view.

2) Roberto has a childish and lively side that comes out when Sara is asleep. What does he hold back from doing at this time?

3) Sara grew up with a lot of prejudices about Naples and its inhabitants. Can you tell some of them?

4) Roberto suggests it takes decision and respect for pedestrians to drive well in Naples. Do you think it's something special or plain common sense?

5) Naples is a source of continuous wonder for the girl. What does she appreciate and stares at?

6) Spaccanapoli. Roberto tells Sara the story about the name of this ancient and renowned road. What does the verb "spaccare" means, then?

7) Roberto makes up a slogan for food in Naples. Can you create a similar catchphrase for your country's food, in Italian?

QUIZ

Choose the right answer among the options.

8) Sara feels embarrassed at the end of the journey, because
1) she couldn't utter a single word.
2) she snored a lot while sleeping.
3) she slept during the entire journey.

9) Sara is amused by
1) Naples loud sounds and reckless driving.
2) the nature and ancient buildings.
3) the pedestrians.

10) Sara's attitude towards driving in Naples is:
1) she wants to try to drive around.
2) she thinks she wouldn't be able to drive in Naples.
3) she's scared of the other drivers.

11) Sara's attitude towards visiting Naples is:
1) she's impatient and curious.
2) she would better rest before exploring the city.
3) she would better have lunch before exploring the city.

12) Roberto absolutely wants Sara
1) to see his flat.
2) to taste the food.
3) to go bathing in the sea.

VOCABULARY

comincia (inf.: cominciare) - start
pulizia - cleaning
banchine - platforms
folla - crowd
barzellette - jokes
metto (inf.: mettere) - put/lay
piede - foot
modo - way
salgono (inf.: salire) - get in
sfreccia (inf.: sfrecciare) - speed
torti - wrong
badare - pay attention
finestrino - window
salita - hill/rise
si allarga (inf.:allargarsi) - stretch out
vorrebbe - would like

CAPITOLO 10:
CHE MERAVIGLIA!

"Aspetta un attimo qui!"

Ma il ragazzo non ha bisogno di insistere: Sara rimane ferma, incantata di fronte alla vista panoramica e non si accorge che Roberto si è allontanato.

Si spaventa quando si sente toccare la spalla: Roberto le porge una ciambella grande e piena di zucchero.

"Assaggia, si chiama graffa. E' uno dei miei dolci preferiti, una specie di frittella, ma ha una morbidezza unica."
Sara mangia con gusto: "E' vero, si scioglie in bocca! Wow!"
"Vieni, ti presento il mio pasticcere di fiducia. Dato che la graffa ti è piaciuta, hai il permesso di conoscerlo" scherza.

"Piacere, Sara."
"Piacere, Giovanni. Ma non sei di qui, eh?"
"No, sono di Milano."

"L'ho notato dalla prima parola che hai pronunciato! Ti piace Napoli?"

"E' la prima volta che la vedo... è davvero incantevole. Il mare, tutti quei palazzi antichi... e poi la sua graffa!"

"Mi piace questa ragazza. Bravo Roberto, mi raccomando... falle fare un bel giro!"

I due parcheggiano la macchina e proseguono a piedi attraverso i vicoli e le strade. Roberto la conduce per le scalinate strette che dividono vecchie palazzine e cortili. Sara non smette mai di guardarsi intorno.

Continuano a camminare per una lunga discesa e Roberto si ferma, indicando un grande edificio dipinto sul lato opposto della strada.

"Questo è un centro sociale. Un gruppo di ragazzi ha occupato l'edificio, che era un ex-manicomio, poi l'ha trasformato in un centro di promozione sociale e aiuto alle fasce deboli e povere della popolazione. Organizzano di tutto: assemblee popolari, assistenza medica e prevenzione, sportelli di assistenza psicologica... E anche serate con musica dal vivo, corsi creativi e di lingua italiana per stranieri..."

"Che meraviglia, si capisce osservando da fuori che è un bel posto, dipinto così. Mi piace tantissimo la street art."

"Qui vicino c'è un altro posto meraviglioso. E' una delle pizzerie migliori di Napoli."

Lo stomaco di Sara brontola, rispondendo all'affermazione di Roberto.

"Ho capito, ho capito, ci andiamo subito!" ride lui.

READING COMPREHENSION

1) Put the sentences in the right order to obtain a short summary of the chapter.
a) The couple starts a walking tour in the city.
b) Sara enjoys the donut and Roberto introduces her to the pastry chef.
c) Roberto stops in front of a big, colorful building and tells its story.
d) Sara feels hungry.
e) Giovanni understands Sara comes from Milan right away.
f) Roberto buys a typical dessert and offers it to the girl.
g) They walk through alleys and streets, staircases and courtyards.

2) Why doesn't Sara notice that Roberto went away for a moment?

3) What makes a Neapolitan *graffa* unique?

4) How does Sara win the honor to meet Roberto's favorite pastry chef?

5) Why does Giovanni like Sara?

6) Roberto tells Sara the story of a colorful building: a former mental hospital turned into a social center by a group of young people. Can you describe the main activities organized by the association? Can you tell their purpose?

7) What does Sara like about the social center?

8) Why does Roberto suggest going to eat pizza right away, at the end of the chapter?

QUIZ

Are the following statements true or false? Mark V (vero) for true and F (falso) for false. Mark NS (non specificato) when not specified in the text.

9) Sara notices Roberto leaving.
- V
- F
- NS

10) "Graffa" is a traditional dessert with the shape of a donut and sugar on top.
- V
- F
- NS

11) Giovanni is annoyed by Sara's origin.
- V
- F
- NS

12) Sara is interested in visiting museums.
- V
- F
- NS

13) Roberto loves the social center as much as the best pizza restaurant in Naples.
- V
- F
- NS

VOCABULARY

aspetta (inf.: aspettare) - wait

si accorge (inf.: accorgersi) - notice

si è allontanato (inf.: allontanarsi) - move away

spalla - shoulder

porge (inf.: porgere) - give

qui - here

parola - word

volta - time

giro - tour

proseguono (inf.: proseguire) - go on

posto - place

CAPITOLO 11:
ALLEGRIA, SOLE...

Sara e Roberto entrano da "Starita", una piccola pizzeria. Il locale è pieno di persone, quindi aspettano qualche minuto e poi si siedono al tavolo.

Lui spiega a Sara che si trovano in una delle pizzerie più antiche di Napoli. Ordina delle montanare, piccole pizze fritte con pomodoro e formaggio, e consiglia a lei di prendere una pizza Margherita: quando è buona, una pizza semplice e tradizionale non ha bisogno di strani condimenti. Secondo la sua opinione, gli ingredienti essenziali sono la manualità del pizzaiolo, il pomodoro e il fiordilatte.

Insieme mangiano godendosi ogni morso.

"La pizza a Napoli è davvero la migliore."
"Sono d'accordo!"

"Grazie ragazzi, buona giornata!" dice il cameriere. E aggiunge, rivolto a Sara: "Signorina, si goda la nostra bella città!"

Sara è sorpresa dall'atteggiamento accogliente e aperto delle persone. Sembrano tutti molto amichevoli e sinceri.

Roberto spiega: "Siamo molto più espansivi e cordiali. Potrebbe succederti di chiedere delle informazioni per strada a una persona e finire a passare la giornata insieme. È il nostro modo di essere, ma il lato negativo è l'invadenza e il disordine. A volte vorresti stare solo, ma rischi di offendere qualcuno. Sono tutti disponibili, ma a volte le persone si rivelano poco serie e inaffidabili."
"Certo, è il lato negativo dell'essere espansivi e accoglienti" osserva Sara.

Sara ammira la vitalità del popolo napoletano e le piace essere circondata da tanta allegria e rumore. Napoli le sembra accogliente e pensa che gli stereotipi positivi sono più validi di quelli negativi: mare, sole e allegria.

Insieme, i due proseguono e attraversano le vie, passando davanti a tante, piccole botteghe che vendono qualsiasi tipo di oggetti.

Sara rimane esterrefatta da tanta varietà e Roberto le spiega: "Qui ognuno si arrangia come riesce e cerchiamo di cavarcela in tutti i modi. Tanti di questi piccoli negozi sono storici, ci sono da sempre."

"Mi piacciono molto le botteghe artigianali. A proposito, sembra un'osservazione strana, ma non ho ancora visto un Mc Donald's!"

Roberto ride divertito, e spiega: "Amiamo il buon cibo tradizionale e costa poco. C'è un Mc Donald's non molto lontano da qui, ma è la terza volta che chiude e si sposta in un'altra zona della città. I napoletani non lo frequentano e solo i turisti ci vanno. Piuttosto, non hai ancora assaggiato un vero caffè! Quanto mi manca quando sono a Milano..."

READING COMPREHENSION

1) Scegli la giusta opzione per completare il riassunto.
Choose the right option to complete the summary.

Sara and Roberto enter a small pizza restaurant and *wait to be seated/sit right away*. He orders some fried pizza as a starter and suggests Sara to order a *simple/elaborate* pizza. The waiter is very friendly and Sara *likes/dislikes* his attitude. Roberto explains her the negative and positive sides of being among *open and welcoming/closed and reserved* people. They keep walking past *small shops/big stores* that *are quite recent/have existed since forever*. Sara notices they haven't seen a McDonald's yet. Roberto explains the food chain is not popular because Neapolitans *love their own food/think it's too expensive*.

2) Naples is home to the most popular Italian dish: pizza. In Roberto's opinion, what's the best way to taste it? What are the key ingredients?

3) Sara is surprised by people's open and welcoming attitude. Why do you think she's so startled?

4) Roberto makes examples of a positive and a negative situation that can occur among Neapolitans. Can you find them in the text?

5) There are a lot of small, curious shops. This gives Roberto the occasion to underline another trait of the inhabitants. Can you tell what it is?

6) Sara notices the absence of food chains. What is the reason why she finds that so unusual, in your opinion?

QUIZ

Choose the right answer among the options.

7) Sara and Roberto eat at "Starita". This is one of the most
1) famous pizza restaurants in Naples.
2) expensive pizza restaurants in Naples.
3) ancient pizza restaurants in Naples.

8) Montanara is a starter that can described as
1) a simple fried pizza.
2) a sort of calzone.
3) an alternative for vegans.

9) If you ask for information from a pedestrian in Naples, you could end up
1) being ignored.
2) being robbed.
3) passing the rest of the day with that person.

10) If you refuse an invitation so you can stay on your own, the other person
1) could feel offended.
2) won't care for sure.
3) will be totally understanding.

11) The positive stereotypes about Naples can be summarized as...
1) pizza, spaghetti and the sun.
2) sea, sun and cheerfulness.
3) pizza, arts and sea.

12) The shops Sara and Roberto pass by are mostly
1) pizza restaurants.

2) small shops.
3) Bakeries.

13) Neapolitans prefer to go out and eat
   1) local food.
   2) at McDonald's.
   3) in ethnic restaurants.

14) The current McDonald's
   1) recently opened their first store in the city.
   2) is mostly popular among tourists.
   3) is having a huge success.

15) Roberto thinks Neapolitan coffee
   1) tastes sometimes too strong.
   2) is nothing special.
   3) is the best Italian coffee.

VOCABULARY

piccola - small
si trovano (inf.: trovarsi) - find yourself
formaggio - cheese
prendere - take/order
quando - when
manualità - manual skill
godendosi (inf. godersi) - enjoy
sono (inf. essere) d'accordo - agree
rivolto (inf. rivolgersi) - address
molto - very
circondata - surrounded
davanti a - in front of
lontano - far
assaggiato (inf.: assaggiare) - taste
quanto - how much

CAPITOLO 12: ...E MARE!

La coppia entra in un sontuoso caffè all'angolo della strada. Le pareti sono piene di quadri e il locale sembra elegantissimo.

"Come preferisci il caffè? Amaro o zuccherato? Se non vuoi zucchero, devi dirlo prima."
"Ah, ma davvero? Amaro, grazie."
"Acqua frizzante o naturale? A Milano sono così maleducati da non offrirla. Ma il caffè va gustato e bisogna pulirsi la bocca con un po' di acqua prima."
"Grazie, che sete!" risponde Sara, finendo il bicchiere in un sorso solo.

Dopo il rito del caffè, i due si fermano in una piazza. Sara la riconosce subito.
"Questa piazza è famosissima! Che meraviglia!"
"Vieni, te la mostro. Questa è Piazza Plebiscito. Le due statue a cavallo che vedi rappresentano due imperatori. Alla tua sinistra vedi Palazzo Reale, mentre il grande edificio dietro al colonnato è la Basilica Reale."
"E' tutto fantastico."

"Il modo più divertente di vedere la piazza, però, è questo!"

Roberto copre gli occhi di Sara e la sfida: "Ok, di fronte a te ci sono le due statue, ricordi? Se prosegui diritto ci passi in mezzo. Ma scommettiamo che non ci riuscirai?"
"Ma sono lontanissime tra loro! E' facilissimo passare in mezzo, basta semplicemente camminare nella stessa direzione."

Sara comincia a camminare e dopo un po' Roberto le toglie le mani dagli occhi. Sara si sorprende quando scopre che sta guardando nella direzione opposta.

"E' una piazza grande, ma è la terza volta che giri in tondo!" ride Roberto.
"Che strano, ero convinta di camminare diritta! Sto camminando al contrario!"

"Proseguendo per questa strada vedremo il mare. Ma voglio portarti in un posto ancora più bello. Vieni con me" propone Roberto.
I due salgono su un autobus che li porta quasi al confine della città. Scendono e proseguono a piedi su una strada panoramica.

"Non siamo ancora arrivati, seguimi!"

Roberto prende una via laterale. All'inizio è ampia e asfaltata, poi continua con un piccolo sentiero in mezzo al verde.

I due si ritrovano in una piccola baia. C'è una spiaggia, l'acqua cristallina del mare e delle rovine che emergono dall'acqua, poco distanti dalla riva.

"Che spettacolo! E' incredibile! La città e, all'improvviso, questo paradiso!" esclama Sara.

"Napoli si può criticare quanto si vuole, ma una cosa così a Milano non esiste proprio..." osserva Roberto.

"Se stai cercando di convincermi a restare qui, non potevi trovare un modo migliore..."

"Davvero? Sei seria? Ci stai pensando veramente?"

Sara tace, il suo volto sorridente è oscurato da un velo di tristezza.

READING COMPREHENSION

1) Scegli la giusta opzione per completare il riassunto.
Choose the right option to complete the summary.

Sara and Roberto enjoy the "coffee ritual" in a *common/luxurious* café. They stop in a *famous/casual* square. Roberto wants Sara to experience the square by seeing it *from above/in an unusual way*. He covers her eyes and invites her to walk *straight ahead/backwards*. Sara starts walking, then opens her eyes again: she's walking in the *same/opposite* direction. Roberto and Sara take *a taxi/a bus*. They walk on a *panoramic/secondary* street, then take a side road. The path ends in a beautiful bay and Sara thinks about *leaving/staying in* Naples.

2) What makes coffee a ritual in Naples? Is it just about the quality of the drink? Does Sara truly enjoy the ritual?

3) The main square. *Piazza del Plebiscito* is the scenery of the main events in Naples. Concerts, national ceremonies and political meetings usually take place here. During Christmas time, contemporary art statues are installed next to the two equestrian statues representing emperors Ferdinando I and Carlo III. They are usually criticized for their eccentricity: you can research the installations over the years and see for yourself!

4) Roberto challenges Sara: what does she have to do? Does she lose or win the challenge?

5) A paradise just outside the city centre. Roberto shows Sara a lovely, hidden place: a bay where the water is crystalline and the ruins of a Roman palace emerge from the sea, near the coast. It's a protected area, called the *"Submerged Park of Gaiola"*: people can relax on the shore, sunbathe and dive. The marine wildlife is incredibly rich and offers a stunning experience.

QUIZ

Are the following statements true or false? Mark V (vero) for true and F (falso) for false. Mark NS (non specificato) when not specified in the text.

6) Pictures are hanging on the walls in the café.
- V
- F
- NS

7) Coffee is a ritual all over the Italian peninsula.
- V
- F
- NS

8) Palazzo Reale and Basilica Reale surround Piazza del Plebiscito.
- V
- F
- NS

9) There's a colonnade in front of Basilica Reale.
- V
- F
- NS

10) Basilica Reale is a church.
- V
- F
- NS

11) Roberto covers Sara's eyes using a scarf.
- V
- F
- NS

12) Sara is sure she's going to win the challenge.
- V
- F
- NS

13) The sea is near Piazza del Plebiscito.
- V
- F
- NS

14) The path that leads to the bay is in concrete.
- V
- F
- NS

15) Sara and Roberto go bathing in the sea.
- V
- F
- NS

16) Sara's face darkens because she thinks about going back to Milan.
- V
- F
- NS

VOCABULARY

maleducati - unpolite
bocca - mouth
prima - before
sorso - sip
però - anyway
scommettiamo (inf.: scommettere) - bet
riuscirai (inf. riuscire) - succeed
basta (inf.: bastare) - be enough
terza - third
seguimi (inf.: seguire) - follow
asfaltata - covered with concrete
cosa - thing
così - like this

CAPITOLO 13:
VIVI IL MOMENTO

"Perchè quell'espressione?" chiede Roberto.

"Sono contenta di essere qui, ma sembra tutto solo un bel sogno."

"Puoi tornare tutte le volte che vuoi, sarai sempre la benvenuta."

"..."

"Goditi il momento e non ti preoccupare. Sai... anche io ho intenzione di continuare a vederti. Troveremo un modo. Intanto goditi questo bel mare..."

Roberto solleva Sara tra le braccia e la butta in acqua, bagnandola completamente.

Sara si vendica e trascina il ragazzo, e insieme finiscono per infradiciarsi i vestiti da capo a piedi.

E' quasi sera quando raggiungono casa. L'appartamento di Roberto è all'ultimo piano di un alto palazzo e dal balcone la vista è mozzafiato.

Dopo una doccia, Sara esplora l'abitazione. In sala c'è un divano comodo e una poltrona verde, occupata da cuscini arancioni e grigi. Non c'è la televisione.
Il corridoio porta a un bagno dipinto di azzurro con una grande finestra, ai cui lati scendono due piante rampicanti.
Lo studio è ordinato e spoglio: ci sono solo una scrivania nera e una sedia blu. Sopra il tavolo c'è un pc portatile con una cover rossa e una piccola lampada, mentre sotto la scrivania, a lato della sedia, è appoggiata una pila di documenti.
La camera è luminosa: una grande porta finestra dà accesso al balcone esterno. Una parete è interamente coperta da una libreria, le altre sono coperte di poster e il giallo delle lenzuola sopra il letto matrimoniale è mezzo coperto da documenti sparsi disordinatamente.

Sara grida: "Ecco chi dorme insieme a te la notte!"
Roberto la raggiunge: "Scusa per il disordine, ultimamente ho dovuto fare gli straordinari al lavoro per sistemare tutto e potermi prendere qualche giorno di pausa... Ma non hai ancora visto la cucina!"

Il ragazzo accompagna Sara in cucina. Mentre lei si faceva la doccia, lui aveva preparato la cena.

"Sei davvero incredibile!" esclama Sara.
"E' una cosa veloce, ma è buonissima e puoi portarne una fetta con te per il viaggio, domani. E' una frittata di pasta, mia madre mi ha insegnato a farla, ma io non sono bravo come lei." risponde Roberto, con modestia.

READING COMPREHENSION

1) After reading the chapter, can you guess what the title means? Do you agree with this motto?

2) Put the sentences in the right order to obtain a short summary of the chapter.

a) Sara takes a shower.
b) Sara is still upset.
c) Both of them get completely wet.
d) Roberto brings her back to the present by lifting her up and throwing her into the water.
e) Roberto shows her the kitchen: he prepared dinner.
f) They finally reach Roberto's flat.
g) The girl explores the flat.

3) Sara is upset, at first. How does Roberto react, at first? What does he do to cheer her up? How does she react?

4) Which floor is Roberto's flat? What can be seen from the balcony?

5) At home. Sara explores the flat in this order: first the living room, then the hallway that leads to the bathroom, a study, a bedroom and the kitchen. Can you tell what she finds in each room? If you find it difficult, proceed to the next exercise, then try again.

6) A colorful place. Sara notices the colors of the furniture and objects in the various rooms as she explores the house.
Learn some colors in Italian by helping yourself with the following statements:

- The armchair is green, occupied by orange and grey pillows.
- The bathroom is painted in light blue.
- There are just a black desk and a blue chair in the study.
- There's a portable pc with a red cover on the desk.
- The yellow color of the bed sheets is half covered with documents.

7) Where is it? Below is a simple table illustrating the sentence structure needed to answer this question. Practice with the words you've learned or try to build sentences with the help of a dictionary.

There is/are	OBJECT	position	the	OBJECT
C'è	OGGETTO	sopra - *on*	il (masculine)	OGGETTO
		sotto - *under*	la (feminine)	
Ci sono		a lato di - *next*	lo (neutral)	

8) Sara makes a joke about the documents that cover Roberto's bed. Can you explain it?

9) When does Roberto prepare dinner? How can he surprise Sara?

10) Frittata di Pasta. It's a traditional Neapolitan dish, originally made with leftovers, that makes a perfect picnic dish and can be enjoyed hot or cold. It's very simple and super tasty: here's a simple recipe for you to try!

INGREDIENTS

300 g spaghetti	100 g smoked pork cheek	black pepper to taste
5 eggs	4/5 tbsp milk	salt to taste
70 g parmesan cheese	extra virgin olive oil to taste	

Whisk eggs together with salt and pepper in a bowl. Add grated parmesan cheese and milk, in the meantime cook spaghetti and leave them firm to the bite: the cooking will continue in a pan. After 7 minutes, you can strain the pasta well and add it to the egg compound together with the smoked pork cheek. Stir well and pour in a nonstick pan with a drizzle of oil, trying to distribute the compound uniformly. Cover and let cook for 10 to 15 minutes on a low flame. Serve hot or cold.

QUIZ

Choose the right answer among the options.

11) Sara makes a strange expression, because
1) she wants to go bathing.
2) she's hungry.
3) it all feels like a dream to her.

12) Roberto tries to reassure Sara by telling her
1) he wants to see her again and they'll find a way.
2) he wants her to be his fiancée.
3) the sea is beautiful.

13) Sara ends up completely wet, because
1) Roberto lifted her and threw her in the water.
2) Roberto pulled her in the water.
3) Roberto dragged her in the water.

14) Sara reacts to Roberto's joke by
1) throwing water onto him.
2) getting angry.
3) dragging him in the water.

15) By looking at Roberto's living room, we can understand
  1) he's a tireless reader.
  2) he's a painter.
  3) he doesn't watch TV.

16) By looking at Roberto's bed, we can understand
  1) he has been working a lot, lately.
  2) he never works at home.
  3) he loves comics.

17) Roberto's dinner dish
  1) can be eaten while travelling.
  2) is an Asian recipe.
  3) is difficult to make.

18) Roberto learned the recipe from
  1) his grandmother.
  2) his aunt.
  3) his mother.

19) Sara is going to leave
  1) we can't say
  2) next week.
  3) the following day.

VOCABULARY

solo - only
sempre - always
intanto - in the meantime
braccia - arms
da capo a piedi - from head to toe
comodo - comfortable
grande - big
rampicanti - climbing
ordinato - tidy
spoglio - spare
luminosa - bright
straordinari - overtime
fetta - slice

CAPITOLO 14:
UNA NUOVA OCCASIONE?

Roberto accompagna Sara alla stazione, la mattina seguente.
"Promettiamoci solo che ci rivedremo presto", propone Roberto.
"Promesso!" risponde Sara con un sorriso, prima di salire sul treno.

Il viaggio di ritorno sembra passare troppo in fretta: tra mille pensieri e con lo sguardo fuori dal finestrino, Sara si ritrova presto in stazione e poi a casa.
Anna non vede l'ora di sentire i suoi racconti, non appena tornerà a casa dal lavoro e le due amiche si rivedranno.

Sara chiama il suo capo e avvisa che rientrerà al lavoro il giorno seguente.
"Che voce da funerale... Sei sicura di essere guarita? Stai bene?" si preoccupa il capo.

"Sì, sì, stia tranquillo. Ho solo bisogno di riposare bene stanotte. A domani!" rassicura lei.

Sara e Anna parlano a lungo: Napoli e Roberto hanno conquistato il suo cuore e lei non sa davvero più cosa fare, si sente confusa e piena di nostalgia.
"Non ho mai incontrato nessuno come lui... E' così bello, pieno di attenzioni, è così pieno di vita..." dice Sara malinconicamente.
"Ti sei presa davvero una bella cotta. Ma c'è una soluzione: prova a trovare lavoro su internet! Ho un'amica che conosce le lingue straniere e lavora autonomamente. E' perfetto per te: non sarai costretta a vivere a Milano e sarai libera di trasferirti a Napoli! Potrai vivere dove preferisci."
"E' una splendida idea!"
"Funzionerà, ne sono certa! In questo tipo di lavoro è importante solo essere determinati: prima o poi qualcosa da fare si trova!"

Sara lavora al bar durante il giorno e non appena torna a casa cerca lavori di traduzione, piccoli o grandi, facili o difficili.

Comincia a ottenere le prime commissioni e lavora con abilità e precisione, attenta a consegnare nei tempi stabiliti nonostante la possibilità di lavorare solo la sera, dopo l'orario di chiusura del bar.

Si accorge che tradurre e scrivere le piace moltissimo ed è piena di gratitudine per l'occasione che la vita le ha offerto.

READING COMPREHENSION

1) Scegli la giusta opzione per completare il riassunto.
Choose the right option to complete the summary.

Roberto accompanies Sara to the station *some days later/the next morning*. When leaving, they *cry/make a promise*. Thinking and looking outside the window, Sara feels her journey lasted *an instant/forever*. Anna is *at work/home* and can't wait to hear about her friend's experience. Sara calls *Roberto/her boss* to tell him she's ok and ready to go back to *work/Naples*. When Sara tells Anna about her travel, the latter suggests Sara can try to find a job *on the internet/in another café* by taking advantage of her *linguistic/bartender* skills. Sara follows Anna's tip and starts working as a translator *after the bar closes/on weekends*.

2) What promise do Sara and Roberto make?

3) Why does Sara's boss think she's still sick?

4) How does Sara feel when she tells Anna about the boy and the city she just left? How does she describe Roberto?

5) What does Anna suggest Sara? How did she come to know about this kind of opportunity? What's the key factor for success in this kind of job?

6) Sara works after her workplace closing time. Do you remember what time does it close?

7) Why does Sara feel gratitude, at the end of the chapter?

8) What do you think about freelance work? Did you or some close friend or relative experience it?

QUIZ

Are the following statements true or false? Mark V (vero) for true and F (falso) for false. Mark NS (non specificato) when not specified in the text.

9) Roberto and Sara find it difficult to say goodbye.
- V
- F
- NS

10) Sara doesn't enjoy her frittata di pasta: she feels too upset to eat.
- V
- F
- NS

11) Anna helps Sara with her luggage at the station.
- V
- F
- NS

12) Sara reassures her boss she'll be ok with a good night's rest.
- V
- F
- NS

13) Anna thinks Sara has a big crush on Roberto.
- V
- F
- NS

14) The best advantage of a freelance job online is the chance to live where you like.
- V
- F
- NS

15) Sara can work online because she possesses a degree.
- V
- F
- NS

16) Sara is fast, precise and skilled when translating.
- V
- F
- NS

17) Sara translates when she has nothing else to do at the cafè.
- V
- F
- NS

18) Sara is not particularly excited about her new side job.
- V
- F
- NS

19) Sara is getting rich.
- V
- F
- NS

VOCABULARY

sguardo - gaze
guarita - recovered
cosa - what
fare - do
incontrato (inf.: incontrare) - meet
costretta - forced
funzionerà (inf.: funzionare) - work
prima o poi - sooner or later
nonostante - despite

CAPITOLO 15:
ADDIO, MILANO!

Con il tempo, Sara diventa sempre più abile e nel giro di un mese ha clienti privati che si rivolgono a lei.

Roberto la segue e la incoraggia da lontano, chiamandola al telefono.

"Continua così! Sono davvero felice per te! E' bello lavorare facendo ciò che ci appassiona."
"Sì! Mi sento fortunata ad averti conosciuto, Roberto... Mi hai aperto nuove prospettive! Non avrei mai pensato di poter lavorare con le lingue straniere."
"Perchè no? Sei bravissima. La passione porta a risultati migliori che lo studio forzato. Sono sicuro che andrà sempre meglio."

Una sera, Sara riceve un'offerta inaspettata.

E' un grande progetto di traduzione, che la terrà impegnata almeno per un anno e le garantirà uno stipendio fisso e stabile. Non crede ai suoi occhi: chiama subito Roberto e lo informa della novità.

"Grande! Che meraviglia! Dobbiamo festeggiare! Ti sto per regalare un biglietto del treno, in diretta..."

Nei giorni successivi, lei e Roberto parlano a lungo dei loro progetti per il futuro.

Il ragazzo pensa che le cose si debbano fare in due: Sara si è impegnata per trovare un lavoro e lui le ha promesso che sarebbe sempre stata la benvenuta, a casa sua.

"So che è una proposta coraggiosa, ma vorresti vivere insieme a me?"

Sara prende il treno la settimana seguente, Anna la aiuta a trasportare i mille bagagli.

"Buona fortuna. Ho fiducia in voi: andrà tutto bene."
"Sì, sento anche io che andrà tutto bene. Vieni a trovarmi presto!"

Il viaggio in treno, stavolta, sembra non finire mai.

Appena scende a Napoli, Sara sente il suono di un clacson. Scoppia a ridere e saluta l'addetto alle pulizie, che esclama: "Signorina, che bel sorriso!"

Roberto le corre incontro, la abbraccia e la aiuta con le valigie.

In macchina c'è una bottiglia di vino e due bicchieri: "Cosa ti ho detto? Dobbiamo festeggiare, signorina traduttrice!"

I due brindano e Sara dice: "Salute! Al mare, al sole e all'allegria!"

READING COMPREHENSION

1) Answer the following questions: they'll help you create a summary for the chapter. If you find it difficult, solve the quiz and the other exercises first, then come back to this one.

a) How is Sara's side job going?
b) How is Roberto's attitude towards Sara?
c) Why does Sara feel incredulous?
d) Why does Roberto think Sara is perfectly able to work as a translator?
e) Sara receives a great offer. Why is the proposal so good?
f) How does Roberto react?
g) Where is Sara going to move?
h) Why does Sara burst into laughter, as she hears a honk?
i) How do Sara and Roberto celebrate their new beginning?

2) Roberto wants to do his part in their life project as a couple and invites Sara to live with him. We don't know about her answer. What do you think this might be?
What would you answer, in her position?

3) Life change. Sara was able to change her life thanks to her strong feelings towards Roberto, together with her passion. She was ready for a change: she didn't like her job anymore and was getting tired of her life. Those elements added up to allow a significant change, together with luck. What about you? Would you like to change your current life? If so, what holds you back? What are your strongest motivations?

4) Salute! Sara toasts to sea, sun and happiness. What would have you toasted to, if you found yourself in their place?

QUIZ

Choose the right answer among the options.

5) Sara works for an increasing number
    1) of friends.
    2) of private clients.
    3) of big businesses.

6) Roberto tells Sara he's happy
    1) she's passionate about her new job.
    2) she's going to move with him.
    3) she's going to study and get a degree.

7) In Roberto's opinion, the best results are met
    1) through forced but necessary studies.
    2) through self-sacrifice.
    3) through passion.

8) Sara receives a great offer: it's a translation project
    1) for a big company.
    2) for a creative novel.
    3) that will last a whole year.

9) Roberto buys her _____ as a present, right away.
    1) a train ticket
    2) a suitcase
    3) a travel to Iceland

10) Roberto thinks that _____ is important in a couple.
    1) individuality
    2) cooperation
    3) sharing the same ideas

11) Anna feels _____ about Sara's future.

    1) uncertain

    2) a bit worried

    3) confident and positive

12) The journey on the train feels

    1) neverending.

    2) boring.

    3) extremely tiring.

13) As Roberto sees the girl, he

    1) runs to her, hugs her and helps her with the luggage.

    2) honks vigorously.

    3) wants to toast.

VOCABULARY

addio - goodbye
crede (inf.: credere) - believe
in diretta - in real time
aiuta (inf.: aiutare) - help
stavolta - this time
bicchieri - glasses

CONCLUSION

You followed Sara's story as she begins as a bartender in Milan, then gets to know a boy from Naples who helps her discover the best sides of his home town. Roberto triggers Sara's will to change her life and makes her see beyond prejudices and her own limits. It's a journey through Italy, a hymn to life and to the determination to change it.

First of all, congratulations for completing the book!

It takes effort and concentration to approach a different language and a strong will and continuous practice to master it.

But don't worry, there's much better news to come!

The best language teacher is the practical experience one acquires by travelling and finding oneself forced to learn because of need.

Those of you who are serious about learning Italian can build up your basics on books, attending lessons and watching videos, but a visit to Italy will make the difference.

Italians are, generally speaking, open and welcoming people and they'll be glad to speak their language with you. There are plenty of websites you can use to find suitable occasions to meet up. Among the most popular is Couchsurfing.com. Why not try sending an invitation to a local? Social media helps as well. The internet has made communication easier and opened a world of possibilities.

Travelling to Italy will act as a great boost for your motivation. It's a country of natural and historical beauties, and a great travel destination that will make you forget about the rest of the world.

Who knows, you could even think about moving in the country of "la bella vita!" As the story tells, sometimes stereotypes can be true, and this is the case, especially in some parts of the country where you could enjoy a warm climate and the sea nearby.

There's another reason to build up your determination to learn Italian. As you get deeper into the language, you discover how rich and fascinating it can be. In the book, you read about two examples that refer to the meaningful historical background that lies beneath the current Italian words.

Think about how centuries of war, passions, faith, arts and creativity made the Italian language what it is now:

- gentle sounds and a great musicality, appreciated almost everywhere in the world;
- a wide range of vocabulary able to express the slightest shade in the universe of human emotions;
- words that draw from the Latin and Greek philosophical worlds, historical cradle of European reflections.

If you're a more practical person and don't really love abstractions... just think about the taste of true Italian cuisine. The language is just as enjoyable as a forkful of handmade fettuccine! (... and ordering them in Italian might make them even more tasteful.)

If you still don't know what I'm talking about, give yourself the chance to experience as a present: no regrets, it's a guarantee!

READING COMPREHENSION AND QUIZ KEYS

CAPITOLO 1: BUONGIORNO!

2) in a café

3) amiche

4) Sara si lava i denti e la faccia, si pettina i capelli e poi va in camera da letto per vestirsi. Prende la borsa con le chiavi, il portafoglio e il cellulare ed esce di casa.

5) early - just loves - late - hurry

6) awake - asleep; early - late; punctual - late

7) 3

8) 1

9) 2

10) 1

CAPITOLO 2: CHE FATICA IL LAVORO!

1) work - late - responsible and punctual - happy - hard - without - messy - flies - same worries

2) 3rd paragraph

4) spazza i pavimenti con la scopa e lava per terra. Pulisce velocemente il bancone - pulire il locale - plus clients service / scuotendo la testa

5) Un caffè lungo e un bicchiere di succo d'arancia, grazie!

6) at 16.30 - at 17.30

7) V

8) NS

9) F

10) V

11) V

CAPITOLO 3: UNA NUOVA ESPERIENZA

1) outside - a friend - free from - accepts - well - bus - beautiful - can't find

2) "Pronto?" - "Come stai? Tutto bene."

3) "Che autobus devo prendere per andare a..?" - Fermata - "In che direzione devo andare?" - "Prenda la prima via a sinistra." - "Giri alla seconda via a destra"

4) "Ciao, piacere di conoscerti, sono (*name*). Faccio la/il (*job*)."

5) curiosa - curious; disorientata - disoriented

6) NS

7) F

8) F

9) F

10) NS

CAPITOLO 4: MODELLA PER UN GIORNO

1) big suitcases - other parts of Italy - clothes - uncomfortable -
marching - musical instruments - run - satisfied with - a lot -
three times

2) clothes

3) Sara is asked to move in front of Debora and the model is
annoyed because Sara is hiding her.

4) "Uno, due, tre... via!"

5) her energy

6) maglietta - I vestiti ti stanno benissimo! - indossa - scarpe -
tacchi alti - pantaloni

7) 3

8) 2

9) 2

10) 3

11) 2

CAPITOLO 5: L'INCONTRO

1) eats a lot - just a bit - leave their personal data and go home - her day - had fun - Roberto - distracted - boy she met - thoughtful - the police

2) camminare - stare in piedi - cadere – correre

3) both eat a lot without getting fat

4) Name: - Surname: - Address: - Phone:

5) his face

6) the police knows her name, the voice sounds familiar

8) 3

9) 1

10) 2

11) 1

12) 2

CAPITOLO 6: PROPOSTA DA PAZZI

1) the police - is happy and - the next day - coffee - café - very concentrated - happy - in the last drawer – dress

2) pazzo - noun: pazzia - means "crazy". the word is used by Roberto to describe Sara's recklessness when she accepts his invitation

3) mi - ti - la - ci

4) tace - chiede - dice - esclama - si lamentano - dettavi - domanda - racconta - si giustifica – spiega

5) è al settimo cielo

6) si sveglia la mattina dopo, più presto del solito e piena di energia. Va al lavoro saltellando, cantando per la strada.

7) she makes lots of mistakes - she is focused and efficient

8) Sara thinks Roberto is the police, Roberto thinks Sara loves elegant clothes

9) 2

10) 2

11) 3

12) 3

13) 1

14) 2

15) 2

16) 2

17) 2

CAPITOLO 7: NORD E SUD

1) c - g - d -a -e -b – f

2) che lavoro fai? - cominciare a lavorare - lavoro nel settore delle risorse umane - mando curricula - faccio la barista - non lavori qui? - cosa hai studiato? - avere un buon lavoro

3) Milan – Naples

4) history, people, climate, sea

6) 2

7) 2

8) 1

9) 3

10) 1

11) 1

12) 2

13) 1

14) 3

15) 1

CAPITOLO 8: VIENI CON ME!

1) lets Roberto convince her - got a bad flu - she sees Roberto's smile - doesn't enjoy her life enough - preparing her breakfast - but can't sleep - Sara's face looks terrible 2) riluttante - indecisa - si sente in colpa - dubbi - felice – impaziente

3) influenza - dottore - ammalarti - ti senti meglio - riguardati

5) V

6) F

7) V

8) V

9) F

10) F

11) NS

12) V

13) V

14) V

CAPITOLO 9: BENVENUTA A NAPOLI!

1) almost immediately - when they arrive at their destination - honk - expected that - feels offended - fast and reckless - pedestrians - lower - higher

2) he would've pulled a prank on her

3) people is loud and drive recklessly

5) nature, ancient palaces, the view

7) break

8) 3

9) 1

10) 2

11) 1

12) 2

CAPITOLO 10: CHE MERAVIGLIA!

1) f - b - e - a - g - c - d
2) because she's staring at the view
3) its softness
4) she appreciates the graffa
5) because she compliments with him for his dessert
6) activities: assemblies, medical assistance, prevention, psychological support, live music, creative courses, language courses - purpose: social assistance and gathering place
7) the artworks on the walls
8) Sara's stomach makes noise
9) F
10) V
11) F
12) NS
13) V

CAPITOLO 11: ALLEGRIA, SOLE...

1) wait to be seated - simple - likes - open and welcoming - small shops - exist since forever - love their own food
2) a simple Margherita - tomato, fiordilatte and the skills of the pizza chef
3) she's used to more reserved people
4) positive: you might find yourself passing the evening with the person you asked information to, people is friendly - negative: you might offend people if you refuse an invitation to stay on your own, people might not be reliable
5) people is creative when it comes to find something to do as a job
6) she's used to see lots of food chains
7) 3
8) 1
9) 3
10) 1
11) 2
12) 2
13) 1
14) 2
15) 3

CAPITOLO 12: ...E MARE!

1) luxurious - famous - in an unusual way - straight ahead - opposite - a bus - panoramic - staying in

2) no. - Coffee is served with sugar and people are offered water to wash their mouth and taste it at its best. - Sara drinks the water because she's thirsty.

4) Sara should walk straight with her eyes covered. No, she doesn't.

6) V

7) F

8) V

9) V

10) NS

11) F

12) V

13) V

14) F

15) F

16) V

CAPITOLO 13: VIVI IL MOMENTO

1) It means "Live the moment"

2) b - d - c - f - a - g – e

3) He tells her he wants to see her again. Then he throws her in the water and she finds it fun.

4) The last floor. A panoramic view.

8) She tells Roberto she discovered who does he sleep with: his work.

10) He makes dinner when Sara is having a shower.

11) 3

12) 1

13) 1

14) 3

15) 3

16) 1

17) 1

18) 3

19) 3

CAPITOLO 14: UNA NUOVA OCCASIONE?

1) the next morning - make a promise - an instant - at work - her boss - work - on the internet - linguistic - after the bar closes

2) They will meet again

3) Sara makes a funereal voice

4) confused, melancholic and nostalgic. She describes Roberto as handsome, full of attentions and full of life

5) Anna suggests Sara to work online. A friend of her works as a freelancer. It takes determination.

6) 17.30

7) she has been offered an opportunity to change her life

9) F

10) NS

11) F

12) V

13) V

14) V

15) F

16) V

17) V

18) F

19) NS

CAPITOLO 15: ADDIO, MILANO!

1) Sara's getting to work for more and more clients.

Roberto encourages her.

She can't believe she could work as a translator.

Roberto thinks passion makes her able to work better than mere studies.

Sara is offered a one-year long translation project that will earn her a decent salary.

Roberto buys her a ticket to Naples as a present right away.

As soon as she arrives to her new city, Sara hears a honk and remembers about the last time she went there

The two toast to celebrate.

5) 2

6) 1

7) 3

8) 3

9) 1

10) 2

11) 3

12) 1

13) 1

A Message from Babel Publishing

Thank you for downloading this book and learning about the beautiful language that is Italian. We hope you enjoyed reading it and are ready to put what you have learned to practice. This is only the beginning but you have now embarked on a journey to discover numerous amazing cultures and encounter wonderful people from all around the world.

We strive to connect people everywhere by removing communication barriers, and we are currently working on other books to help people learn about other languages such as French, Portuguese, Japanese, Spanish, German, and more. To ensure we provide the best learning experiences possible, we would love to get your feedback so we can provide you and other readers with the quality you all deserve. Please share your experience with us and other readers by leaving a short review on Amazon.com.

Thank you and Arrivederci!

Babel Publishing

118